PAUL FORRESTER.

A PLAY IN FOUR ACTS.

NEW YORK.

1871.

CHARACTERS.

MICHAEL FORRESTER.

PAUL FORRESTER, *his son.*

ADOLPH DE BEAUBERG.

LEA DE CLERS.

CAMILLE, *cousin to* LEA *and ward of* MICHAEL FORRESTER.

JAMES }
JOHN } SERVANTS.

PAUL FORRESTER.

ACT FIRST.

Interior of Paul Forrester's Studio. Doors centre, right, and left. A large canvas on an easel. Paul and John discovered. Paul painting, and John arranging the different things about the room.

Paul.

LET those things there alone ; go down stairs and see,
Be quick, if there are any letters for me.
[*Exit John.*
Without one word or sign for three days and more,
Our quarrels were never so lasting before ;
But now that the fault is all on her side,
The effect of caprice, perhaps of false pride,
Delight in my agony she seems to see,
And waits thus for humble repentance from me ;
Is it that our union less worthy appears,
And, to complete her joy, need she have my tears ?
Or, tired of love, does she hope to tire
My love ; and, in absence, slake my desire ?
Could I think Lea false, I should hate her name
For trying me thus and thus fanning my flame.
What means then this silence ?

[*Enter John*]. *John.*
I've a letter here.

Paul (*taking letter hastily*).

I was sure she would write. 'Tis not from Lea.
(*Crushes letter and throws it down.*)
[*Exit John.*
Oh hard-hearted woman, is there then no trace
Left of pity for me in that lovely face?
'Tis food for your caprice you'd seek, and would dare
To brave my hot tears, my disgrace, my despair.
But you shall wait in vain for such proof from me,
My tears, my despair, my disgrace, you'll ne'er see.
I'll wait till you come, should you never return,
And, if it must be so, from my breast I will spurn
All trace of your false love ; but you shall not see
How profound that love, how deep that agony.
[*Enter Forrester.*]

Forrester.

Good day, Paul.

Paul.

Good day, father.

Forrester.

Ah ! what is wrong ?
Your eyes are on fire, your breath quick and strong.
What's the matter ?

Paul.

Nothing. It seems all in vain.
I can't work as I should. It wears on my brain.

Forrester (*goes to Picture*).

Let's see ! Rather weak, that Milo, rather weak.
Give more force to the arm, more hue to the cheek.
Or he'll seem but to tear the bark from the tree,
You have given him strength : he lacks energy.

Paul.

I shall never gain that force which has named you
Michael Angelo.

Forrester.

Don't despair. It is true
That my name is Michael ; those who add the rest
Think that they flatter me ; a thing I detest ;
Let me, as a sculptor, counsel you, my son,
Since sculpture and painting are too much for one
Man to practise in these days ; I'll join my strength
To your weakness, thus you'll meet success at length.

Paul.

Weakness you never had.

Forrester.

How should you know, pray ?

Paul.

You moulder of marble and bronze as mere clay !
What can you know of that, you who are as bold
In talent, and firm as the statues you mould.
Your genius, so strong, so intense, and so pure,
Develops itself in those things which endure.
While mine is so fitful, so weak and so tame
That darkens obscures even its brightest flame.
I shall never succeed.

Forrester.

If you would be great
Strive as Pygamalion strove ; so strive to create.
For that which the Greeks, in their fable of old,
Teach us, modern art speaks in language more cold.
In the arts none can serve two masters, my son.
At your age I'd made choice for myself of one.
All illicit pleasure I boldly ignored,
And found that in virtue lies its own reward.

Paul.

More easy to give than to take—such advice.

Forrester.

No, a happy marriage shields man against vice.
Without woman's love of what worth is this life ?
Why, our griefs are half griefs when shared with a wife,
It is woman's mission, in marriage, to prove
A harbor of refuge in her sacred love.
Strive hard with yourself and time itself will cure
Those passions of which the mere thought is impure.

Paul.

You suspect me !

Forrester.

I do.

Paul.

Can you then believe ?—

Forrester.

My son, there are signs which can never deceive
A father's eyes. That same hard strife with your art
Proves that some strange Goddess now reigns in your heart.
When, like Samson, shorn of his locks, you appear,
'Tis safe to assent that Delilah is near.
If such women contributed to success
Or to our mental strength—

Paul.

To that even less
Than the other.

Forrester.

We sacrifice for their sake
All, because we give all.

Paul.

And because we take
Nothing in return.

Forrester.

They destroy manly pride.

Paul.

Make sure of their triumph, then cast us aside,
Our vows turn to jests, our affections deride :
And then, finding some man who pleases them more,
Boldly discard the first and vote him a bore ;
Ask him what has put such ideas in his head,
The next time they meet, with a smile, cut him dead.

Forrester.

'Tis true.

Paul.

Women have no hearts now-a-days.

Forrester.

They had in my time.

Paul.

How well you know their ways.

Forrester.

You are in love, Paul.

Paul.

No. 'Tis true I did think
Myself loved, when I only stood on the brink
Of a dark precipice, whose depth I now see
With dread, and with hate, of its foul perfidy.

Forrester.

Are you sure ?

Paul.

Can we love those whom we despise ?

Forrester.

I've heard of such things.

Paul.

Among fools—*I'll* be wise.

Forrester.

I know it is easy for parents to preach
To their sons, but 'tis not so easy to teach
Other hearts. Of proverbs most true, this is one :
It is a wise father who knows his own son.
But I know your heart, and feel sure when you say
The thing must be done—

Paul.

That I'll soon find the way.

Forrester.

Come, confess the truth. What's her station in life ?

Paul.

Much the same as our own. She's rich.

Forrester.

Ah, the strife
Of fashion and wealth has quite taken away
Those feelings in which this fast world of to-day
Leaves no time to indulge, for women we know
Live less for their homes than they do for mere show.
Flattery, love of dress, indulgence, applause,
With the sex of our day, are the only laws.

Paul.

My burthen has become too heavy for me.

Forrester.

Then promise me, when once from this burthen free,
To renounce such folly and marry—yes, both.

Paul.

I will swear to do so.

Forrester.

I accept your oath.

[*Enter Adolph.*]

Adolph.

Adolph de Beauberg.

Forrester.

My old pupil, your hand !

Adolph.

Old master ! And Paul ! I am yours to command.

Forrester.

Our what ?

Adolph.

Any thing you may please, my old boy,
Your pupil, your model, your slave, your post-boy,
(*picking up letter which Paul has thrown down*)
Take care of your letters.

Paul.

(*Looking at Postage Stamp.*) 'Twas posted at Nice.

Forrester.

From Reynal ? (*Paul motions " Yes."*)

Adolph.

What news do you get from Maurice ?

Paul.

He's ill.

Adolph.

I hope soon to be with him again.

Forrester.

Ah, when ?

Adolph.

I leave Paris by this evening's train.

Paul.

You leave ?

Adolph.

Emigrate.

Forrester.

And you go ?

Adolph.

Anywhere,
For I'm bored !

Forrester.

And your friends ?

Adolph.

They cannot much care.

Forrester.

You travel for business or pleasure ?

Adolph.

I'm bored,
Must have change.

Forrester.

And this change you would seek abroad.
For shame ; why, a handsome young fellow like you,
With great lots of spare cash and nothing to do,
With talent almost, pray, wherefore should you roam
Strange lands for those conquests you'll find nearer home ?

Adolph.

You'd like to know why ?

Forrester.

Yes, I should ; speak out—well ?

Adolph.

I'll confess to you, now, if you will not tell.
You think me, perhaps, a great rake ; that I go
To escape from the women, do you ?

Forrester.

Oh, no!

Adolph.

Indeed, you surprise me. If I don't mistake
All the women believe me a gay, young rake.

Forrester.

I never remarked it.

Adolph.

How prudent you are!
But, if you suppose it, believe me you're far
From the truth, my friend ; for, would you believe so,
My greatest of faults is timidity.

Forrester.

No!
Perhaps, my young friend, you've not tried the right sort.

Adolph.

I've tried them all, young, old, fat, lean, tall and short.

Paul.

Madame de Clers, perhaps?

Adolph.

Why, how could you know?

Forrester.

Lea!

Adolph (to Paul).

Who told you?

Paul (embarrassed).

(*Aside.*) I felt sure it was so.

Forrester.

Such practices you should not have indulged here,
In my house.

Adolph.

But--

Forrester.

You've been imprudent.

Adolph.

Look here!
Now Madame de Clers' no relation to you.

Forrester.

My pupil—my niece—or, almost so.

Adolph.

That's true;
But no blood relation, so you cannot claim —

Forrester.

I'm a very old friend—that's almost the same.
And Paul here and she have long loved each other
As I'd have them love—like sister and brother.
Where old friends are concerned, it has been my pride
When trouble came on them, to stand by their side.
Now, it so turns out, as you are well aware,
That among those old friends is Madame de Clers.
And, when that wretched man, her husband, did force
Her to demand her rights, and seek a divorce,
'Twas I who did furnish the means to defend
Those rights, and throughout all her grief, stood her friend,
And exposed, in spite of the world, my gray hairs
To those accusations which calumny dares.

Adolph.

You're the same old, hot-headed chap, as of yore.

Forrester.

I defended virtue against vice.

Adolph.

No more,
I beseech ! In this one case you are quite out,
And you do not know what you're talking about.
If you'd but have patience, you'd very soon see
That, instead of blaming, you should pity me,
For she, most persistently, turns a deaf ear
To my prayers.

Forrester.

I'm glad to hear it.

Adolph.

Lea
Is not—

Forrester.

Change the subject. You mean to confess,
(*slapping him on the back*).
Your modesty stands in your way to success ?

Adolph.

Yes, except with women of a certain class,
I'm nervous, and timid and modest, alas !
And then I've pitched my standard so very high,
That I can't find what I want, in fact I sigh
In vain ; for the woman that I choose must bring
Beauty, innocence, and all that sort of thing.

Paul (*laughing*).

Pray Heaven preserve you from such a sad fate.

Adolph.

I'm in a sufficiently well preserved state
Already. So long as I'd hope of success
I never told any body my distress.

Forrester.

You despair ?

Adolph.

I do.

Forrester.

Don't say so.

Adolph.

I'm so frank.
I know that I have only myself to thank
For it all.

Paul.

Ah !

Forrester.

Why so ?

Adolph.

I'm so timid, or—
Modest.

Forrester.

I think I heard you say so before.

Adolph.

You see that I open my whole heart to you.
I do wish to goodness that I only knew,
How you approach the sex.

Paul.

Why, much as you might.

Adolph.

I'll tell you what happened to me but last night.
You must know then I'm never happy unless
I'm in love with some dancer or some actress ;
Well, one of these ladies, who's very well known,
An acquaintance of mine, asked me for a loan :
A pretty large sum, which I thought rather cool,
And said so. She called me a mean, vulgar fool,
And turned on her heel. What do you think of that ?

Forrester.

I'm no judge of such matters.

Adolph.

Well, now, that's flat!
So, *you* think me a fool?

Forrester.

I did not say so.

Adolph.

No, not quite; you intimated it though.
Well, if I am timid, and modest, and plain,
Which I doubt—'tis my parents must bear the blame.
I really can't help it, for I've done my best,
Spent plenty of money, am always well dressed.
But I give it up, and shall now emigrate.

Paul.

You might try once more; it may not be too late.

Adolph.

My talents you none of you appreciate.

Paul.

Your lot's very hard. You must blame it to fate.
Or, if you insist upon fighting the fates,
Just make a journey to the United States.
Foreign noblemen are much thought of out there—
At least so I've heard.

Adolph.

Oh, of that I'm aware.

Forrester.

You're modest, and rich, and if more things you need,
You've a title; with that you're sure to succeed.

Adolph.

You give me an idea.

Forrester.

Just think of the use
Such talents might serve ; the effect they'd produce.

Adolph.

I'll make up my mind to set out on the spot.

Forrester.

I think you'd be much to blame if you did not.

Adolph.

Yes, I'll cross the ocean. And just take a look
At America. I come back, write a book ;
It will be sure to take.
[*Enter Camille*].

Forrester.

Camille !

Camille.

Even so.
Pardon that I thus invade your studio.
(*Presents her forehead to Forrester, who kisses her.*)

Adolph (*to Camille*).

I'll bid you good-morning. I'm off now. Good bye.

Forrester.

Adieu, gay young rake.

Paul.

Adieu, Lovelace.

Adolph.

O fie !

[*Exit Adolph*].

Paul.

Bon voyage !

Camille.

Where's he going ?

Forrester.

Adolph sets out
In search of adventure.

Camille.

He'll return ?

Forrester.

No doubt !
Was that question prompted by interest or whim ?

Camille.

I don't know, I'm sure.

Forrester.

You don't admire him,
And you're right. Well, this is your first holiday.
How shall it be spent ? Shall we leave Paul to say ?

Camille.

I should like of all things to dine with Lea.

Forrester.

You and Paul shall go and dine with her, my dear.

Paul.

Quite impossible.

Camille.

Why ?

Paul (embarrassed).

I'm engaged—you see—
With some friends.

Camille.

Won't you give them up to please me ?

Paul.

No, I really can't, though I don't care a bit
To go.

Forrester.

You said nothing to me about it.

Camille.

How thoughtless !

Paul.

I forgot.

Camille.

It was unkind, Paul.

Forrester.

At least you'll accompany her, and will call
Later.

Paul (to Forrester).

I go to *her* house ?

Forrester.

Why not ? and bring
Camille home.

Paul.

Are you sure it would be the thing ?

Forrester.

I'm not very well. Martha's busy, and so—

Camille.

Well, John can take me, I'm sure you need not go.
And since Paul has other engagements, meanwhile—

Forrester.

Very well.

Paul.

John's gone out.

Forrester.

Indeed ?

Camille.

Why that smile ?

Forrester (*to Paul*).

Well then, you *must* go, since he's out and I'm ill.

Paul (*aside*).

At least she shall know I went against my will.

[*Exit Paul.*

Camille.

Poor Paul, all these visits seem against the grain.

Forrester.

You're mistaken, my dear. Well, now, to be plain,
You asked me just now why I smiled ; well, forsooth,
Because John's down-stairs and Paul told an untruth.

Camille.

With what object ?

Forrester.

Why, bless you, you little elf,
Because Paul wanted to go with you himself.

Camille.

But then, why not say so ?

Forrester.

He is shy, you see.

Camille.

Indeed !

Forrester.

Does the thought displease you ?

Camille.

No.

Forrester.

Nor me.

Camille.

But, yet, why refuse ?

Forrester.

He thought you might suspect
What he was about ; but to change the subject,
Have you ever thought of your sad position ?

Camille.

Sad !

Forrester.

Of your orphan, dependent condition ;
You have scarce a friend now save myself and Paul.

Camille.

And is not that enough ? have you not been all
A fond father could ? Is not Paul my brother ?
(*Laying her hand on his shoulder.*)
At least I'm certain we love one anothe

Forrester.

Bless your little heart. I'm quite sure that you do,
And that brings me to what I would say to you.
You see, darling, I'm getting old and infirm,
And shall very soon have attained that term,
Beyond which we cannot hope to remain here ;
No, don't look so sad and down-hearted, my dear,
'Tis the fate of all men ; and certainly I
Can't be an exception : all that live must die.
After my time this will be no home for you,
And you'll understand it is equally true
That, according to the immutable rule,
You cannot pass your whole life at boarding school.

Camille.

No, that, I of course, very well understand ;
There's but one way left—marry me out of hand.
What do you say to that ?

Forrester.

Well, where shall we find
A husband in all respects of the right kind
For you ?

Camille.

Paul would do.

Forrester.

What, who, Paul ?

Camille.

Yes, he.
I know that you have always wished it might be.

Forrester.

How stupid of me to beat about the bush
As I did ! How a true woman's heart will rush
To its end ! Yes, darling, the aim of my life
Has been, before I died, to see you Paul's wife ;
My complete happiness but one thing has lack'd :
The becoming, through Paul, your father, in fact.
'Twas your mother's last prayer on her lone death-bed,
When calling down blessings from heaven on your head.
And 'twill be my last prayer.

Camille.

Your last prayer, you say ?
And what prevents that prayer being granted, pray ?
'Tis for me to obey, for you to command.
As for Paul—

Forrester.

Ah, Paul !

Camille.

Do you think he'll withstand
Your will ?

Forrester.

We must sound him.

Camille.

Must sound him, why ?
Surely he knows your wish quite as well as I.

Forrester.

Then he's spoken to you ?

Camille.

On this subject—no ;
But your word is his law, as 'tis mine, you know.
For us to marry strangers would never do ;
It would be but to separate us from you.
A thing I'd not think of.

Forrester.

'Twould be hard in truth,
If, after having passed together your youth,
You could not unite in this old heart, which you
Know, beats but for the happiness of you two.
In your loves my youth will return back to me.

Camille.

When shall we marry ?

Forrester.

When Paul's heart's again free.
When I say his heart, I'd have you understand
That I mean when he's done his work now on hand.
For you know how he is wrapped up in his art ;
And now that alone rules supreme in his heart.
Once more free from her toils we need have no fear
Any other will rule but our goddess here.
'Tis he (*listening*).

Camille.

Then I'm off.

Forrester.

Not a word !

Camille.

I can't seek
Him now, or myself be the first one to speak.

[*Exit.*

Forrester.

Oh you sly little puss, who would have supposed
You loved Paul all the while, yet never disclosed
Your love ? Womankind, what enigmas you are !
We think ourselves wise, but 'tis plain that you're far
Wiser than we. In deceit, hypocrisy,
You are very much more apt scholars than we.
You call us the lords of creation, 'tis true ;
But, in knowledge of hearts, we must bow to you.
Pray heaven that Paul's heart again may be free ;
For I know that young soul, with its gayety
And joy, holds a depth of affection so rare
That to lose his love were more than it could bear.
If Paul, to our grief, should have formed other ties,
As I sometimes have feared, then it with me lies
To use that authority which, until now,
I have never made use of, and make him bow
To my paternal will. Ah, 'tis hard to prove
That labors like these are mere labors of love.

(*Turning to picture.*)

He does not work now as he has worked of late,
His color and drawing are less accurate.
Let me see if I cannot, from the source
Of my stronger power, give his thoughts more force.

(*Taking up Paul's palette and turning to the picture.*)

[*Enter Lea stealthily, withdrawing the key from the door and putting it in her pocket.*]

Lea.

Since the mountain won't come to Mohammed, he
Must just come to the mountain.

Forrester.

What do I see?
(*Aside.*)

Lea.

His father!

Forrester.

You here?

Lea.

Good heavens!

Forrester.

I am free
To confess this meeting surprises me more
Than my words can now give expression to, for,
Of all women who might have led Paul astray,
You are the last I should have suspected; nay,
My past services in your behalf afford
Proof that might have met with a better reward.

Lea.

I've deceived you.

Forrester.

Lea, if fault ever did
Call up all my deep sympathy and forbid
Censure, it is yours. There's been so much to blast
All your hopes of happiness in the sad past.

Lea.

Oh, how good you are, how good, how merciful;
Yet have I great need of all your bountiful
Charity. For I'm like some wretched outcast,
Like some storm-tossed ship, without rudder or mast,

Deprived of Paul's love—and yours. Possessing that
I'm strong to resist the world's scorn and its hate.

Forrester.

Such pity I give as of friendship is born.
My pity you have; my pity, not my scorn.

Lea.

My loftiest aim and my happiest dream
Was, winning his love; to win your esteem.
Since you condemn me not, is there need that I
Fear the shafts of envy and of calumny?

Forrester.

'Tis not my voice condemns, but 'tis the command
That speaks trumpet-tongued in the law of the land.

Lea.

The law of the land?

Forrester.

Yes, in solving the tie
Which bound you for life, it gave not liberty
To form other ties, for that decree enforced
All those pains which fall on a woman divorced.

Lea.

While Paul's love for me lasts, he and I can wait.

Forrester.

While it lasts; but may you not find, when too late,
That the sentiment which now your hearts does move
Was more passing passion than enduring love?
Do you feel such faith in its force and its truth
To think it will outlive the fancy of youth?
And that, in after years, respect will succeed
That love, which it ought the rather to precede?
And can you trust to time, that slayer of all
Things mortal, to strengthen your claims upon Paul?

Were you now free, as you hope one day to be,
I should force myself to be content and see
You Paul's wife, and all those cherished dreams resign
Which, through long years past, have not ceased to be mine.
When, now in your strong hope, you say you can wait,
Do you realize those awful words, "too late ?"
May not those dread words rise up some day and blast
Those fond dreams of love, so unlikely to last ?
For many years Paul will still be young, while you—

Lea.

Must soon grow old. The words are cruel, but true.
And when that sad time comes I can but expect
To find his indifference and his neglect ?
Neglect which would leave me alone, desolate.

Forrester.

Not only you'd have his neglect, but his hate.

Lea.

Oh no, say not so, for when that day had come,
No selfish passion should defile the dark tomb
Of our love. No sigh should be heard, and no tear
Should e'er meet his gaze, no complaint greet his ear.
My sorrow I'd hide in my heart ; and, unseen,
It should live on that happiness which had been.

Forrester.

No, memory is not the only support
Of age ; for when, from the past we seek comfort,
'Tis one thing bears us up, and one thing alone ;
That consoling sense of a duty well done.

Lea.

But I have no one to claim duty from me.

Forrester.

All ranks have their duties, if they could but see
Where they lay; and it often happens that those
We think farthest off are, in fact, the most close.
So, in our Paul's life, you would prefer to share
As angel of hope rather than of despair.
Ought you not for him to shun the precipice—
Not in passion triumph, but self-sacrifice?

Lea.

You'd have me give up Paul?

Forrester.

'Tis what I wish.

Lea.

No,
I must not, I can not, I will not do so.
Your fatherly love is too selfish by far.

Forrester.

All true love is selfish.

Lea.

In that our loves are
Alike. Must mine be all the sacrifice, and
Yours all the triumph?

Forrester.

Your most just reprimand
I accept.

Lea.

You men, sir, are all just the same,
Misfortune befalls you, and sorrow and shame;
A victim is needed and, since your sex can
Not yield, why of course it must be the woman.
And our force to suffer must grow with our years;
To you all the smiles and to us all the tears.

Forrester.

Ah, speak not of sacrifice to these gray hairs ;
Little you know what sacrifice has been their's.
He, who now of you this great sacrifice begs,
Has drained that bitter cup quite down to the dregs.
The truth of that heart, which we both struggle for,
Proves I've loved more wisely, if not loved him more.

Lea.

More wisely and more ! but I defy their proof.

Forrester.

By its strength of sacrifice I judge love's truth.
From the time that his mother died, and I stood
Alone, I have sacrificed all for his good.
Our union had not been happy, and so,
In a second marriage, I then sought to know
That happiness which I had longed for in vain,
That happiness, my only hope, my sole aim.
I had loved your dear mother, my cousin, and
Once more being free, I again sought her hand.
Ours was not a thoughtless, wild, passion of youth,
'Twas founded on reason, self-sacrifice, truth.

Lea.

You were both worthy of such an union,
And I fail to see how it could harm your son.

Forrester.

The gay heart of youth has strange ways of its own ;
No sooner did this plan of mine become known
To Paul, and he saw that another must stand
In the place his mother had filled, and command
His duty, than he became sad and downcast,
Neglected his studies, his playmates ; at last
Fell ill, so severely ill, that now the strife
Had become a battle between death and life.

Your mother and I watched his bed night and day,
Through many long weeks, in which my poor child lay
Thus in his delirium and his unrest ;
But one idea alone seems to have possessed
His mind ; and, with anguish, he'd cry night and day :
" Oh why should you drive my dear mother away ? "
This cry of his filled my sad cup to the brim ;
That place, to me vacant, was ne'er void to him.
In my selfish love I would have cast aside
That love, which had ne'er ceased to be his heart's guide.
Between inclination and duty the strife
Was a hard one ; it seemed to hold my whole life.
The temptation was far too much for my strength ;
But she, with true woman's perception, at length
Saw my weakness, and, in her strength, dared to stand
On our duty, and then rejected my hand.

Lea.

After having so lost your life's paradise
Indeed you may well speak of self-sacrifice.

Forrester.

Not alone of sacrifice, but of reward.
For, however that sacrifice had been hard,
The satisfaction was quite without alloy
When I knew his gratitude and his great joy.
Ah, it is sweet to see those whom we love gain
Their happiness through our denial and pain.

Lea.

If denial and pain must rise from our love,
Mine be the denial, mine the pain to prove
Its purity. I place my fate in your hands,
And bow down in the future to your commands.
For myself I ask nothing, so do your worst,—
But will he not suffer when I'm gone ?

Forrester.

At first,
No doubt he will suffer. Trust to time to cure
The wound. 'Tis of all other means the most sure.

Lea.

I now understand his long absence of late ;
'Twas intended, no doubt, to facilitate
A rupture ; and you've undertaken as his
Ambassador—

Forrester.

No, he knows nothing of this.

Lea.

How know you then that Paul's love may not outlive
This trial ? How know you it may not deprive
Him of hope, of all ; or, eternal remorse
And regret for ever, embitter the source
Of his life ? It is not my own cause I plead,
But his, for I well know how great is his need
Of my love. Mere absence will not break the tie
That binds us.

Forrester.

I think that it will. Let us try.

Lea.

If this trial of yours should fail of success,
Will you then give way to my claims on him ?

Forrester.

Yes,
Provided 'tis made in good faith.

Lea.

I accept
The test. Your conditions shall be strictly kept ;
For, in yielding myself, your pardon I win.
Speak, what shall I do ? Where am I to begin ?

Forrester.

Leave Paris.

Lea.

Well ?

Forrester.

And you must not let him know
Which way you are gone. You must even do so
Without meeting again.

Lea.

Oh no, that I can
Never do.

Forrester.

Then that puts an end to my plan.

Lea.

What will he think if I abandon him thus ?

Forrester.

Nothing that to your love can be dangerous,
Trust me. Unless you part there is not enough
To test his constancy, and therefore this proof.
Such love as you speak of, must be but a jest
If it cannot withstand the proof of such test.
And how can he or can you credit its truth
Unless by your absence you put it to proof ?
The doubt which in your hesitation is shown
Lays bare those suspicions your lips dare not own.

Lea.

When will the term of my exile be complete ?

Forrester.

I'll send you word.

Lea.

You ?

Forrester.

I attempt no deceit.

Lea.

Will he ever forgive you ?

Forrester.

You must allow
That it is not *his* cause you are pleading now.

Lea.

I tremble.

Forrester.

You fear to put him to the test :
I have no more to say.

Lea.

No, I yield. It is best
I should go.

Forrester.

Thanks.

Lea.

I set out at once.

Forrester.

May He
Who reads your inmost heart guide your destiny.

(*Embraces her.*)

END OF ACT FIRST.

ACT SECOND.

A room in Forrester's house, handsomely furnished. Doors Right, Left and Centre. Paul, Camille and Forrester discovered. Paul on his knees painting Camille's portrait, who sits for the purpose. Forrester stands behind Paul, watching him at work.

Paul (*to Forrester.*)

She has certain lights and shades I cannot seize.

Camille.

Oh, I'm ugly then !

Forrester.

No.

(*Camille rises and approaches Paul.*)

Paul.

Well ?

Camille.

Just one peep, please.

Paul.

Ah, you naughty child, to your place, and don't stir.

Camille.

I will have some recompense, then ;

(*Draws his head back and kisses him on the forehead.*)

there, now, Sir !

Paul.

To your place.

Camille.

What tyrants these husbands are.

Paul.

Thanks.

Forrester.

Are they not ?

Camille.

Downright brutes.

Paul.

Silence in the ranks.

Camille.

What, not talk ?

Paul.

No, it is your mouth I am at.

Camille (*with closed lips*).

I may listen, then ; now, you won't prevent that ?

Paul.

You may.

Camille.

Then tell me the news, papa, I'm mute.

Forrester.

About what ?

Camille.

About Lea's dreadful lawsuit.

Forrester.

Now that her husband's dead, his family claim
All that she had to live on.

Camille.

Oh ; what a shame !

Forrester.

But their lawyers propose a compromise, and,
'Tis ever my rule, that a bird in the hand

Is worth two in the bush ; or, as it is said :
'Tis better to have half a loaf than no bread !

Paul.

Will you decide, yourself, while Lea's away ?

Forrester.

I have telegraphed, and look for her to-day.

Camille (rising).

Oh, how nice ! We shall once more see her dear face.
What do you say, Paul. Ar'nt you glad ?

Paul.

To your place !

Camille.

Oh !

Paul.

I've no time to think of things of that kind.

Camille.

After just five months—out of sight, out of mind.

Paul.

I've a wife now, what have I to do with *her* ?

Camille.

Though you may not love her, I love her still, Sir.

Forrester.

I thought your happiness full without that.

Camille.

No.

I have no one to talk to about it.

Forrester.

Oh

Fate ! Even mother Eve could do nothing less
Than let out the secret of her happiness.

But, would it be well while her sorrow's so new,
To speak of your happiness ?

Camille.

Is it not true
That Lea's life was sacrificed to that man ?

Forrester.

True, but does that not prove—as far as we can—
That, for those who have heaven's blessings, 'twere best
Not to parade those gifts to others less blest ?

Paul.

The delicacy which you show, in this case,
My dear father, would seem to me out of place.
The indifference of our fair friend for both
The dead and—the *living*—seems equal, forsooth !

Camille.

Her affection for you, you know, is devout.

Paul.

Your happiness then will charm her, beyond doubt.

Forrester.

Let by-gones be by-gones.

Camille.

I hope that she won't
Ask me any questions.

Paul.

But, if she should, don't
Scruple to tell her, what you know is quite true,
That, in your husband's heart, there's room but for you.

Forrester.

What's the matter with you ?

Paul.

What do you blush for ?

Camille.

Paul never said any thing like that before.

Paul.

Don't move ; that is just the expression I want.
Look, father. Oh, if I could only transplant
That look to my canvas. Ah, now it is fled
Quite away ; something else must be tried instead.
Go, quick, change your head-dress, we'll try the effect
Of some other color.

Forrester.

If I might direct,
I'd change the position, or, to be more plain,
I'd begin the portrait all over again.

Camille.

I think you are right. Paul has done too much
To make me look pretty.

Forrester.

Stop, I said no such
A thing.

Camille.

I wish I was as ugly as sin,
And that you thought me lovely.

Forrester.

My love, you're in
A strange humor to-day.

Paul.

Are you not aware,
That heaven has granted one half of your prayer ?

Camille.

Which half, Sir ?

Paul.

Never mind, go and change your dress.

Camille.

Which half, I must know ? Am I ugly, Sir ?

Paul.

(*Kissing her affectionately*) Yes.

Camille.

Oh, you story-teller ! (*patting his cheek*).

Forrester.

Be off, then !

Camille.

I fly !

[*Exit, kissing her hand to Paul.*]

Paul.

O ye women ; heigh ho !

Forrester.

Well, Paul, why that sigh ?

Paul.

Indeed, I don't know ; I am vexed, ill at ease,
Discontented, perplexed ; nothing seems to please
Me to-day. Every thing seems bent to annoy
Me ; I'm weary of life.

Forrester.

You're bilious, my boy.

Paul.

No, 'tis not the stomach ; 'tis the heart, the mind,
That are out of order. I hate all my kind,
Despise human nature. What blind fools are we
To build thus on quicksands, and fondly fancy
That what seems truth, is truth, because we are told
So, and that all which glitters must be pure gold.
There's but one thing lasting, but one thing a part
Of Eternity's self—'tis Art, only Art.

Forrester.

Ah ; you are partly right and yet partly wrong.
All true art is one of those things which, among
Others, outlive time ; but 'tis not art alone
Can fill up our whole life ; Art cannot atone.
For the loss of all else. You seem to forget
Her who has just left us, whose influence yet
Seems to linger behind to dispel our gloom ;
Whose bright smile ever welcomes us to our home.

Paul.

No, truly ; is she not my wife ?—I love
Her for her guileless heart, her faith, but above
All else for the peace which she brings this home, where
All dead hopes are forgot.

Forrester.

Where all grief and care
Are dispelled by her happy face.

Paul.

Ah, yes, true.

Forrester.

Why, my son, she's just the companion for you.

Paul.

For us both.

Forrester.

For us both ?

Paul.

You may well rejoice
In the happy result. My wife has *your* choice.

Forrester.

Was she not *your* choice, then ?

Paul.

Oh ! well, for my part,
It did not matter much, but you'd set your heart
On the marriage.

Forrester.

It surely was not for me
That you married Camille ? Remember how she
Had worshipped us both.

Paul.

Yes, that worship contained
Revelations for me ; for when you named
Camille as your choice, her name called to my mind
My great debt of gratitude ; and that, combined
With my filial love, then made me forget
My own wishes in yours.

Forrester.

What !

Paul.

It was a debt.

Forrester.

A debt ?

Paul.

I'd long owed, and at length the day
Had come, which I'd prayed for, in which I could pay
That debt. I had not forgot the sacrifice
Made to my heedless youth, my thoughtless caprice ;
And I plainly saw that, in choosing Camille
To be my wife, I should contribute to heal
The wound I had caused. By conferring the right
To claim her as your child I thought that I might
Again unite that bond once severed by me,
And for your sake—

Forrester.

Sacrifice yourself, I see.

Paul.

Oh ! 'twas not much.

Forrester.

Heaven will bless you, my son,
For, in seeking my happiness, you have won
Your own.

Paul.

True love's often crushed, but seldom dies.

Forrester.

Say not so ; for Lea, in breaking the ties
Which bound you then to her, may have done, who knows,
You a great service.

Paul.

Greater than you suppose.
Much greater ; she taught me to value aright
All the truth of her sex.

Forrester.

But, might not her flight
Have been prompted by real affection for you ?

Paul.

What, affection for me ? Is it not then true
She abandoned me without even one word
Of farewell ?—ay, truly,—but I can afford
To forget all that ; let it pass.

Forrester.

You're severe
In your judgment, my son.

[*Enter Camille, followed by Lea.*]

Camille.

Come in ; papa's here.

Paul (aside).

Lea !

Lea (aside).

Paul !

Camille (aside).

As I thought !

Forrester.

Forgive my surprise
At your sudden return.

Lea.

Did you not advise
Me to come back at once ?

Forrester.

Yes, of course, my dear,
But I did not expect to receive you here ;
In fact, your opponent himself has not come.

Lea.

I suppose I may wait. Will this troublesome
Lawsuit never end ? Much rather than prolong
It I'm willing to suffer loss, right or wrong,
And yield to his demand.

Forrester.

If that is the case,
The matter's soon ended.

Lea.

Yes, let right give place
To might, and let's end it.

Forrester.

I fear you must wait
Some time yet ; our appointment was fixed for eight,
And it is not six yet.

Lea.

Ah, well, 'till he come
I'll talk to my niece.

Camille.

And to your nephew, whom
You have not yet addressed.

Lea.

My nephew ?

Camille.

Why, yes,
Of course !

Forrester.

You know Camille's married ?

Lea.

Married ?

Camille.

Bless
You ! two months ago !

Lea.

What ?

Forrester.

Did you not receive
My letter ?

Lea.

What letter ?

Forrester (aside to Camille).

I hope you'll believe
I would have spared you this.

Lea.

My nephew, in fact !
I congratulate you.

Paul.

My happiness lacked
But that to be complete ; it makes full amends
For the past.

Lea.

Ah, the past ! But we may be friends,
May we not ?

Paul.

Why not, pray ? such friendship as we
Must feel, is such friendship as men rarely see.
A friendship so lasting, so true ; the effect
Of such confidence, such esteem, such respect !

Lea.

I heard of your marriage, but I did not know
You had married Camille : I'm glad it is so.

Forrester (*to Lea*).

Yes, of course, Paul, of course. (*Aside*) This will never do.
You've not seen this portrait (*showing Camille's portrait*).

Lea.

Camille's, oh how true ;
How speaking !

Camille.

Mr. Paul, you see I was right ;
You said it was ugly.

Paul.

'Tis a downright fright.

Lea.

Your husband is right, my dear, if you compare
The picture with yourself.

Camille.

Oh, fie, Aunt ! how dare
You flatter me so ?

Lea.

He painted mine once, and
Thought it ugly at first.

Paul.

At that time my hand,
Like my heart, was too trusting, too bold ; in truth,
It possessed the foolish reliance of youth.
'Tis time and experience which overthrow
All those false delusions : I know better now.

[*Enter James.*]

James.

A gentleman waits, Sir, to see you below.

Forrester (*aside*).

He has arrived at last.

Lea (*aside*).

'Tis time I should go.
(*Aloud.*) Let us see him at once, I will not detain
You longer. (*To Paul*) Good day, Sir.

Camille (*kissing her*).

Pray come soon again.

[*Exeunt Forrester, Lea and James.*]

Camille.

Why so silent, Paul, eh ?

Paul (*to Camille*).

O innocence, youth ;
O unlimited faith, O unbounded truth ;
O bright angel of peace, of quietness, rest,
Of all that is purest, of all that is best,
Such, such are your titles !

Camille (laying her hand on his shoulder).

You have forgot *love.*

Paul (breaking from her).

That there should be others,—great heaven above !
All falsehood, treachery ; all fraud and deceit,
Like some fair, shining pool, which, down at your feet,
Looks so peaceful and calm ; but only to cheat
The eye, while, below in its foul depths, the while
Lie adders and vermin ; things loathsome and vile.

Camille.

Why, Paul, what's the matter ?

Paul.

And yet 'tis too true
There are men who'd prefer such coquettes to (*to her*) you.

Camille.

Of whom do you thus speak ?

Paul.

Of some friends of mine
Not a thousand miles off.

Camille.

Might I then assign
To Adolph de Bauberg—

Paul.

Why not ? Let us say
'Tis of him that I speak.

Camille.

Oh, Paul, my love, nay ;
I think you are unjust.

Paul.

Well, perhaps I am.

Camille.

We know our friend Adolph's a thoughtless young man ;
But have you not remarked that he's much changed of late :
That he's now more subdued, more staid, more sedate ?

Paul.

No, I've not, 'pon my word.

Camille.

Indeed, it is so ;
Adolph de Bauberg is—

[*Enter Adolph.*]

Adolph.

The proverb, you know,
Says : Speak of the—

Paul.

Angels and you hear their wings.

Adolph.

But then you were talking of quite different things,
I am sure, were you not, Paul ? tell me.

Paul.

Oh, no,
We were talking of nothing.

Adolph.

If I'm *de trop*,
I'll be off.

Camille.

No, pray stay.

Adolph.

Well, then, you'll resume
Your conversation ; and, if I might presume
To ask you its object—

Camille.

Yourself.

Adolph.

No ?

Paul.

Yes,

Adolph.

Pray
What of me ?

Camille.

e were just beginning to say
That, like angels' visits, your visits were few
And far between.

Paul.

That's it.

Adolph.

How kind. It is true
I have slighted my friends ; but I'm a changed man.
Oh, my dearest friend, Paul, conceive if you can
The most perfect woman that you ever saw.
Such hands, and such feet, and—

Camille.

I'd better withdraw.

Paul.

I think you might as well.

Adolph.

Will you pardon me,
My intrusion just now ?

Camille.

Perhaps—let me see—
If you won't keep him long.

Adolph.

Ten minutes, no more.

Camille.

I'll give you just twelve and a half.

Adolph.

Au revoir.

[*Exit Camille.*]

Adolph.

I want your advice ; before I tell the cause
Though, which has brought me here, I'll just shut the doors ;
For it's a great secret.

Paul.

I think I can guess ;
You're in love, are you not ? Am I not right ?

Adolph.

Yes ;
Over head and ears.

Paul.

Ah, that is deep indeed !

Adolph.

You mean that my ears are so long ; pray proceed.
Call me just what you like : you mean I'm an ass
For my pains.

Paul.

No, I don't.

Adolph.

Well ; we'll let that pass ;
I don't mind.

Paul.

That is not what I had to say,
But I've remarked, of late, that you have a way,

When you're in a scrape, of asking my advice,
Which I strongly suspect is but a device
To confirm your folly.

Adolph.

Ungrateful ! for shame !

Paul.

If I share your misdeeds I won't share the blame.

Adolph.

Have I not always asked your opinion, hey ?

Paul.

Yes ; then always have gone the opposite way.

Adolph.

Accidents will happen, but this time I swear
To be guided by you.

Paul.

If so, the affair
Must be serious indeed.

Adolph.

More than serious.

Paul.

A matter of life and death, eh ?

Adolph.

Don't discuss
It in that flippant way.

Paul.

Well, then I'll be grave.
Tell me all about it.

(*Taking his arm and walking up and down slowly.*)

Adolph.

You know that I have
A susceptible heart.

Paul.

So I've heard you say.

Adolph.

After that last affair I could not well stay
In Paris. I went to seek some gayer place.

Paul.

How did emigration agree with your case ?

Adolph.

Why, at first, not at all ; but, after a time,
I became reconciled. With a heart like mine
One can't always be sad. Well, then, at Berlin,
I met such a charmer ; but if I begin
To describe her charms I shall never have done.

Paul.

Then pray don't.

Adolph.

No, I won't ; and then there was one,
A Russian, at Munich ; such eyes, and such hair,
Such a bust, and such feet, and such—

Paul.

We'll stop there.

Adolph.

I wish I had stopped there.

Paul.

Indeed, (*aside*) so do I.
Well, what of the last one ? get on !

Adolph.

I'll try
To describe her.

Paul.

Never mind.

Adolph.

Over head and ears
I fell. For a time she was deaf to my tears,
To my prayers, to my vows.

Paul.

Only for a time !
So the Frauline had you ?

Adolph.

She was no Frauline ;
But a real Parisian.

Paul.

With *real* hair and eyes—
And all the rest ?

Adolph.

Stop, Paul, no jokes ; otherwise
I've done.

Paul.

I am mum.

Adolph.

Be quiet, if you can ;
To give her a name—let's call her Marianne.

Paul.

Why not Sally Ann ?

Adolph.

I declare, you'd disgust
The best fellow alive.

Paul.

Well, then, if you must
Have your way, call her Mary Ann by all means.

Adolph.

If I could but recount to you all the scenes
Of our love.

Paul.

No, don't; I'll take them all on faith.

Adolph.

I'll not describe to you how I dogged her path;
Followed her everywhere, and lived in her sight
Alone; how I dreamed of her form day and night.
How my appetite failed, and how I lost flesh.
My buttons fell away, and how every fresh
Day brought only fresh grief; I, quite a changed man,
Lived only on air, on one word—Marianne!
At length the day came, and we met—'twas by chance,
The usual way, you know; I asked her to dance:
'Twas a waltz. Shall I ever forget that taste
Of heaven, when I put my arm round her waist
And pressed her close to me! Oh, 'twas like a dream!
And then, afterwards, how my joy was supreme
When we walked in the grove, alone by the Rhine,
How, in spite of myself, and without design,
My arm stole about her; she did not resist
My tender advances; and then how I kissed
Her lips and her eyes and—

Paul.

Well, let the rest go,
We all know what followed.

Adolph.

You don't.

Paul.

I guess.

Adolph.

No

You can't ; well, what was it, say ?

Paul.

I'd rather not.
There are things done which are not spoken of.

Adolph.

What
You would insinuate is quite wrong, for when
My joy seemed complete, and she yielded, why—then
She sprang from my arms, wildly hastened away,
Shrieking " I am revenged, and I hate you ! " Say,
Can you explain that ?

Paul.

Yes, 'twas the reaction
Of gratified love, or else the distraction
Of a lunatic ; but you pursued, of course.

Adolph.

No, I didn't.

Paul.

Why not ?

Adolph.

To tell truth, remorse
Had seized me.

Paul.

Oh, nonsense !

Adolph.

But, 'tis a fact.

Paul.

Ah!

Adolph.

And besides, I felt the want of a cigar.

Paul.

'Twas only a dream, then, and when you awoke
Your hot love, like all love, had vanished in smoke.

Adolph.

No, it was not all smoke; the fire still burned
That consumed me; but can you tell why she spurned
Me away as she did?

Paul.

Yes, I have told you.

Adolph.

You're wrong. 'Twas that she had loved another, who
Had been false to her.

Paul.

Oh!

Adolph.

And this was the way
She took her revenge.

Paul.

Did I not hear you say
That this was her home?

Adolph.

Yes.

Paul.

Her name?

Adolph.

Marianne !
I said so before.

Paul.

Ah, of course.

Adolph.

If you can,
Now, guess what followed next.

Paul.

I've had quite enough
Of your guessing. Get on !

Adolph.

Well, my strange rebuff
Had driven me wild, and I wandered the street
All that night, in spite of the rain and the sleet,
Without an umbrella or overshoes, quite
Wet through and through—down to the skin.

Paul.

Served you right !
There's no woman worth that.

Adolph.

The walk cleared my head.

Paul.

And quenched your flame, eh ?

Adolph.

No, I went home to bed,
But not to sleep one wink ; and when mid-day came,
I dressed with great care, and again sought the same
Street I'd walked in all night. I had but one aim :
To see her. I approached the house ; there she sat,
At an upper window ; I took off my hat ;

But she saw me not, so I rang; was struck dumb
By the servant's reply—"Madam's not at home."
I withdrew crestfallen, but soon I came back;
All in vain; 'twas no go. I had got the sack.

Paul.

Vulgar, but no doubt true!

Adolph.

Then my appetite
Told me 'twas dinner-time.

Paul.

And you dined.

Adolph.

You're right,
I did; and dinner done, I went out once more
To try my hard luck. When I came to her door
'Twas shut, and so was the whole house, and there met
My gaze these four dreadful words: "This house to let."

Paul.

She'd thrown you over.

Adolph.

I went straight off home
And wrote; it would have moved the heart of a stone
To read all that I wrote—so tender, so long,
Full thirty-two pages.

Paul.

That was rather strong.

Adolph.

It took a long time, but in my eagerness
I'd forgot that I had not got her address.

Paul.

What a pity that you should take so much pains
To spoil paper and ink.

Adolph.

To blow out my brains
I resolved.

Paul.

That was rash.

Adolph.

Perhaps it was, but
I took up my pistol, approached the glass, shut
My eyes, and with them shut I then tried to find
The right spot to shoot—then—

Paul.

Then you changed your mind.

Adolph.

No, nothing of the sort, Sir, and as a proof,
I pulled at the trigger ; it wouldn't go off.
My fates refused to help me out of my scrape.

Paul.

How very unkind.

Adolph.

I'd a narrow escape,
Had I not ?

Paul.

Truly, yes.

Adolph.

Well, what do you say ?

Paul.

To what ?

Adolph.

To Marianne.

Paul.

Excuse me, I pray,
From expressing my mind.

Adolph.

She is nothing less
Than an angel.

Paul.

An angel ? Of some sort, yes !
But there are two sorts.

Adolph.

Well, then to the point !
Shall I marry or not ? Now don't disappoint
Me by saying "No."

Paul.

Where's the use ? Why should I ?
She's free ?

Adolph

A widow !

Paul.

A widow ?

Adolph.

Husbands die,
Sometimes, do they not ?

Paul.

Ah, yes. Is he long dead ?

Adolph.

No, quite recently.

Paul.

Then this woman has led
You to Paris. You know where to find her ?

Adolph.

Yes,
I have seen her this morning.

Paul.

I think I guess
Her true name. It is not Marianne.

Adolph.

It may
Perhaps be something else.

Paul.

I must know some day,
So then why not confess ? Now out with it.

Adolph.

'Tis clear
You must know some day.

Paul.

Well, her name is—

Adolph.

Lea.

Paul.

Ah ! (*aside*) I knew it was she.

Adolph.

Well, your advice, Paul ;
Shall I marry her, eh ?

Paul.

Why ask, after all
My advice, when you've made your choice ?

Adolph.

You're unkind
To say so.

Paul.

You've already made up your mind.
So go, take my blessing.

Adolph.

Now, I want your aid
In the matter.

Paul.

My what ?

Adolph.

I'm really afraid
To ask her myself.

Paul.

I regret much to say
That I can't interfere. Some one comes this way ;
So let's change the subject.

[*Enter Forrester.*]

Adolph (*to Forrester*).

Ah, how do you do ?

Forrester.

I'm quite well, I thank you, and pray how are you ?

Adolph.

Oh, I'm only so-so. I'm awfully bored.
I'm in love.

Forrester.

When did you return from abroad ?

Adolph.

Only this very morning.

Forrester.

This morning! that
Is odd.

Adolph.

What the deuce have I done with my hat?

Forrester.

When you went you said you should make a long stay.

Adolph.

Yes, but then—well, you see—

Forrester.

You're off?

Adolph.

Yes, good day.
I'm in haste.

Forrester.

Good evening.

Paul (aside to Adolph).

Mind you let me know
The result.

Adolph (aside).

Why should you care?

Paul.

But I do.

Adolph.

Oh,
Very well; *au revoir.* [*Exit.*]

Paul (laughing).

Ha! ha! ha!

Forrester.

Why, Paul,
What is the matter?

Paul.

Father, did you not call
Lea spotless, and pure, and innocent ?

Forrester.

All
This I did.

Paul.

Oh, wonder of purity, grace,
Of innocence, virtue ! Oh, most lovely face,
With nothing but modesty stamped on thy brow !
Whose look was so open, so honest, that thou
A bright angel seemed ! Well, all this innocence,
All this pure modesty, was but a pretence.
A pretence I say. A pretence to entice
Men to believe her pure, and cover her vice.
Within this very week she has yielded, and
To whom do you think ?

Forrester.

I do not understand
You, Paul.

Paul.

And no wonder, for were you to guess
Even ten thousand times, you'd have to confess
Yourself beaten at last. Who do you suppose
Has shared in her pure love ; who was it she chose
To stand in my place ; to whom has she given
All her innocent love, herself ? Why, even
To that fine gentleman who just now stood here,
To that puppet, that fool, that thing !

Forrester.

Poor Lea !

Paul.

There was but one thing lacked to my full content,
And I have got it now.

Forrester.

Such a sad event
Fills me with grief.

Paul.

And it fills me with joy, for
I reproached myself with being hasty ; nor
Could reconcile my mind and feel quite at rest,
With my hasty marriage.

Forrester.

All is for the best
As it is.

Paul.

Without doubt.

(*During this scene Lea has entered unperceived by Forrester and Paul, followed by Camille, and stands hesitatingly. Paul sees Camille without seeing Lea. Camille flies to his arms.*)

Paul.

To my heart, my wife ;
To my heart, and lie close ; henceforward my life
Is your own.

Camille.

Dear husband !

Paul.

We'll leave the deceit
And falsehood to others. Our joy is complete.

(*Camille sinks into a chair, covering her face.*)

END OF ACT SECOND.

ACT THIRD.

A room in Lea's house. Covers on furniture and chandelier, as if the room had been long uninhabited. Lea and James discovered. Lea sunk in a chair, with her arms hanging listlessly. James, on his knees, lighting the fire.

James.

'Tis out of all reason to grieve as you do
For a man, whom all the world very well knew,
Was a hard-hearted wretch, and one who defied
All decency, and who, when he died,
Did the only right thing he'd done in his life ;
Of course it is requisite, being his wife,
To wear mourning for him, if only to thank
Him for dying so soon. I know that your rank
Requires that you should, but then it's all stuff
To cry in this way. I'd see him hanged—

Lea.

Enough !
You forget yourself, James.

James.

Oh, do pray forgive
An old servant, whose heart breaks to see you live
As you do now, without more life than a stone.
Ever since last night you've sat here all alone,
And you might have been frozen for all you care,
With the fire all out, and the winter air

As cold as December, and you like a block
Of ice. You forbade me to wind up the clock,
So that you might forget the course of time, or
Bring you a light.

Lea (starting up).

There's a ring at the door ;
If it's Monsieur Adolph, pray send him away ;
Tell him I'm very ill, or else you may say
I'm out.

James.

I understand quite well, for you told
Me before. One need not be deaf tho' one's old.
[*Exit.*]

Lea (sinking into her chair).

At length I'm quite alone, and life, all a blank,
Lies before me. Oh, why was it that I drank
Of its draught, which the blush of sorrow and shame
Has called up to my cheek ? Where, where's my fair name ?
Where are all my proud hopes, where my faith, my trust
In myself ?—All blasted in hate and disgust.

[*Enter James.*]

James.

Tis Madame Forrester.

Lea.

Well, what does she want ?

James.

She asked for madame.

Lea.

You must say that I can't
See her now.

James.

Very well (*going*).

Lea.

No, stop ! Show her in.

[*Exit James.*]

Now, poor, helpless woman, your strife must begin
With yourself. Oh heaven, do but grant me strength
For that strife !

[*Enter Camille.*]

Camille.

I intrude.

Lea.

Oh ! Camille, at length
You're my guest.

Camille.

Dear Lea ! I said I should come.

Lea.

Did you ? I'd forgot. Well, now we are alone,
Let me have a good look, because yesterday
Id no time to see you.

Camille.

Am I much changed ?

Lea.

Nay,
You're improved ; but when I look at you again,
You are pale ; you look sad.

Camille.

I do not comp lain.

Lea.

You are not happy then ?

Camille.

Not happy ? oh, yes,
Most happy.

Lea.

Ah, indeed ?

Camille.

Could I then be less
With a husband who loves me, and me alone,
And who never has loved any other one ?

Lea.

Is it so ?

Camille.

Yes ; and yet I can't understand
Paul. One moment he is all affection, and
The next he is cold. There, let us not speak
Of me, but of yourself. Now I look, your cheek
Has lost its former hue.

Lea.

Yes, I did not sleep
Much last night. I had many sad thoughts to keep
Me awake. It is no doubt the change of air
Does not suit me ; but then, you know the affair
Which brought me to town is ended ; that alone
Detained me. This evening I'm off.

Camille.

So soon !

Lea.

Yes, I left my servants and my things behind
At Venice. You're happy then ?

Camille.

Yes—I'm resigned
To my fate.

Lea.

To your fate resigned ! Why, Camille,
There is something that you would try to conceal
From your friend.

Camille.

No, not so.

Lea.

You have then found out
That married life is not all brightness ? No doubt
Some cloud has arisen to hide your bright sun.
You are jealous.

Camille.

Not I.

Lea.

And some other one
Shares your love, is it so ?

Camille.

No, Paul is as true
As ever.

Lea.

Perhaps then he *never* loved you ;
But some former love may still burn in his heart ;
And it is this secret which you would impart
To your friend, is it so ?

Camille (*starting up*).

It is false, for he
Has never loved other than me—only me.

Lea.

Did he tell you this ?

Camille.

Yes, 'twas he told me so ;
And I know it is true.

Lea (aside).

Oh heaven, this blow
Might well have been spared me ! (*Aloud*) But then why confess
Any doubt ? Do *I* envy your happiness ?
Do *I* seek to steal it, or do you believe
Me jealous, perhaps ? Speak ! why try to deceive
Me when you cannot ?

Camille.

No, I swear to you, no !

Lea.

Then why—

Camille.

'Twas because that I dreaded to show
My happiness.

Lea.

And why ?

Camille.

I feared to recall
Your happiness and bring back to your mind all
You had lost, all you mourn for ; and I would spare
You that grief—that is all.

Lea.

Oh, Camille, dare
I ask for your pardon, here, humbly, for all
I've said. So Paul loves you ? Let us talk of Paul.
So he loves you alone ?

Camille.

Yes, why should I doubt
His affection? I, who could not live without
That affection? Am I not his wife? Although
That alone is no reason, I very well know.
In these wicked times, there seems something which drives
Men to love strange women, rather than their wives.
I know not what it is.

Lea.

May you never know—
Disappointment, distrust, or deceit. And so
Paul loves you?

Camille.

Yes, indeed. I don't mean to say
That he never has flirted with others, nay,
That would be folly; but of this I'm quite sure,
There never was love more selfish and pure
Than his love for his wife.

Lea.

'Tis the only one
That endures; when past love has been overthrown
And crushed down under foot, then the weak man flies
To married life and strives to live down the lies
Of the past. It is not he who suffers: oh,
It is not he who dies a living death, no!
'Tis not he who's branded with the cold world's blame.
That which should make him blush for him is no shame.
He goes his way proudly, leaving all the weight
Of his crime to his victim—she who, too late,
Wakes up from her bright dream. But why should he care?
Who pities the poor foolish woman? who dare
Fight *her* battle for her? No! no such fear checks
Him; 'tis the privilege alone of his sex
To deceive.

Camille.

Why, Lea, how strangely you speak!

Lea.

It may seem strange to you; but, Camille, this weak,
Down-trod, woman may bear a knowledge so deep
In her heart of hearts that its presence may keep
Revenge warm. The *mistress* may pity the *wife*,
For true love can be known but once in a life.
But, enough, you said you were happy.

Camille.

Oh, yes;
I think so now.

Lea.

Heaven bless your happiness!
[*Enter James.*]

Lea.

Well, what is it, James?

James.

There's a person below
Who says he's your lawyer, but I doubt it.

Lea.

Show
Him up here presently.

Camille.

Goodbye, I must leave
You now.

Lea.

I am sorry. Goodbye, dear.

Camille.

Believe
Me sincere when I say, wherever you go
May Heaven bless you.

Lea.

Shan't we meet again ?

Camille.

No.

I shall not return home again 'till quite late,
For I have an engagement to celebrate
The birthday of a friend.

Lea.

How pleasant, whilst I
Fly away from my friends.

Camille.

Goodbye, dear !

Lea

Goodbye !

[*Exit Camille, after kissing Lea.*]

Lea.

Gone ! How long, oh how long, must this struggle last ?
All is robbed from me now. Not even the past
Remains.

[*Enter Adolph.*]

Lea.

You, sir, here ?

Adolph.

Yes, dear Lea, forgive
My subterfuge.

Lea.

Leave me.

Adolph.

Alas, would you drive
Me mad ?

Lea.

What do I care ! Withdraw, Sir, I say,
Or let me withdraw.

Adolph.

Stay, dear Lea, pray stay.
One word !

Lea.

Am I mistress here, Sir, or are you ?
Leave the room, Sir, I say.

Adolph.

I cannot but do
As you bid. But I came to ask pardon, and
To offer you my fortune and my hand.

Lea.

Your hand
You offer *me* marriage ? Of all others who—
You offer *me* marriage.

Adolph.

Yes, Lea, 'tis true.
Yes, Lea, it has long been my fondest dream.
If you would but consent, indeed I should deem
Myself blessed. What, you weep ? Why those tears ?

Lea (*weeping.*)

These tears
Are not tears of sorrow. Let them flow. For years
I've known no such relief as they bring my heart.
These are tears of gratitude. Yes, they impart
A strange feeling of peace. Oh, little you know
How I've craved sympathy, or even the show
Of outward respect, which the hard world denies
To a suspected woman. Such tears, these eyes
Have long been a stranger to. Let them flow on !

With them one half of my great anguish is gone.
How I've yearned for sympathy and for respect
None can tell.

Adolph.

Now, you cease, I trust, to suspect
My motives.

Lea.

Oh, yes.

Adolph.

You no longer accuse
Me ?

Lea.

Oh, no, I thank you, but still must refuse
Your hand.

Adolph.

You refuse my hand ?

Lea.

I must.

Adolph.

And why ?

Lea.

Ask me not, it is so. Let that suffice.

Adolph.

I
Fear you still doubt my truth. Now you are unjust
To question it still, dear Lea. Then what must
I do to convince you ? I swear that I love
You, and only you. Alas, how can I prove
My affection, when you doubt my words, and when
I offer my hand. Am I repulsive, then,
To you ?

Lea.

No, believe me ; but this thing cannot be.
I thank you profoundly, but—

Adolph.

Some mystery
Lies hid under all this, which I must unveil.

Lea.

Seek not to unveil it.

Adolph.

Why not ?

Lea.

'Twould avail
You nothing.

Adolph.

How cruel, with a single breath
You utter my sentence. That sentence is—

Lea.

Death !
Perhaps you would say ?

Adolph.

Lea, let us not jest.
In this heart you have woke up all that is best
And purest. Nay, Lea, when you are absent,
I am not half myself ; but, when you are present,
I'm more than myself. When you drove me away
Last from your door I, who am always so gay,
Became gloomy and ill. You find this hard
To believe ; but 'tis true.

Lea.

Poor fellow.

Adolph.

And reward
Is there none for such grief ?

Lea.

Yes ! There ! you shall be
My brother.

Adolph.

Oh, thanks ! that won't satisfy me.

Lea.

You shall be my friend.

Adolph.

No, that will not suffice.
All or nothing ! See, on my knees I pray. (*Kneeling.*)

Lea.

Rise.
You shall not kneel to me. Must I then lay bare
My heart's dearest secret ? Indeed, you're not aware
How much you ask me for. Were I to disclose
My secret you'd hate me.

Adolph.

Never.

Lea.

You suppose
That you hold the first place in my heart.

Adolph.

Of course
I think so.

Lea.

You are wrong.

Adolph.

Impossible !

Lea.

Worse :
I have never loved you.

Adolph.

And yet—

Lea.

You would say
That I told you I did. True, but on that day
I had lost all I loved. 'Twas but memory
Of all that I had lost which then prompted me
To fly to your arms. Now you see what contempt
And what scorn I deserve. I make no attempt
At excuse: I have none.

Adolph.

No need; by heaven!
A fault confessed is already forgiven.
I offer you my hand again. Yes or no?

Lea.

I must not accept it; were I to do so
I should bring down a curse. Heaven could not bless
Such an union.

Adolph.

But, Lea, my happiness
Depends only on you. Let other men's aim
Be to win their first love. To me such love's tame.
Give me none of those staid, prim, timid, demure,
Half-developed school-girls; something more mature
Is my dream.

Lea.

Can it be some example that
Some friend has set you? Can you then not look at
Others' joy without envy?

Adolph.

Yes, you are right,
I envy another. That envy the sight
Of Paul's love has produced.

Lea.

Ah, Paul! Is he then
So happy?

Adolph.

Why, he's the happiest of men.

Lea.

Is it so?

Adolph.

Without doubt. Why, to see his wife
And him together, you'd suppose his life
Had known no other.

Lea.

Enough! Let me see.
I'll consider.

Adolph.

Oh, joy!

Lea.

And now, pray leave me
Alone for awhile.

Adolph.

What, you drive me away
From all that I prize?

Lea.

Yes, enough for the day
Is—

Adolph.

The bliss thereof, eh?

Lea.

Yes, in case you will
Have it so. Now leave me.

Adolph.

'Twill seem long until
We meet again.

Lea.

Au revoir.

Adolph.

Will you compel
Me to go ?

Lea.

Yes, you must.

Adolph.

Goodbye, then. [*Exit.*]

Lea.

Farewell.
They are happy, those two. Yes, Paul and Camille
Are happy ; he said so. Why should I not feel
Happy too ? So I will. Paul's happy ! The sight
Of my grief is nothing to him ; he has quite
Forgotten the past. Well, then, let me forget
The past too. Let it be as if we'd ne'er met.
In wedding this man, may I not perchance find
That peace which I've long sought ? Those bonds which shall bind
Us, I here freely take ; and swear to protect
His name, and raise up for it love and respect.

[*Enter James.*]

James.

Mr. Paul Forrester, madam.

Lea (*starting*).

Ha ! (*aside*) So ! So !
You'd brave me, Mr. Paul ! You come *apropos.*

(*To James.*) Show the gentleman up. [*Exit James.*]
So, you'd interfere
Where you've no longer right!

[*Enter Paul.*]
Paul (*aside.*)

Why should I come here?

Lea.

To what may I owe this new honor, Sir, pray,
This unlooked for pleasure?

Paul.

Madam, I obey
A duty. Permit me to explain.

Lea.

Pray do,
For I'm free to confess, Sir, that in our new
Relations I see nought that can justify
This token of respect.

Paul.

You're right, madam, I
Have said that I call'd as a duty. A friend
Has charged me to ask for your hand.

Lea.

He could send
No better messenger! I think I can guess
His name. It is Adolph de Beauberg, then?

Paul.

Yes.

Lea

He has just left my side.

Paul.

You received him, then ?

Lea.

So it seems.

Paul.

He's been here ?

Lea.

So it seems ; and when
You came in he went out.

Paul.

Indeed, had I known
That he'd been here himself, I should not have thrown
Myself thus in your way. Without doubt the match
Is made up ?

Lea.

Well, you know Adolph's a great *catch !*
How could I refuse him ?

Paul.

And then such a choice
Speaks so well for your heart. It must still the voice
Of reproach.

Lea.

Of reproach ?

Paul.

Pardon if I speak
Too frankly.

Lea.

Not at all. I beg you won't seek
To dissimulate.

Paul.

But if I were to say
All I know, I might call a blush—

Lea.

A blush, eh!
A blush, sir, and why? Is it insult you would
Fling at me? Insult me then, Sir.

Paul.

Yes, I could,
But I'll not.

Lea.

Oh, pray do.

Paul.

You're Adolph's mistress,
That's enough.

Lea.

I would that I were.

Paul.

Don't profess
Innocence to me.

Lea.

And pray, Sir, by what right
Do you judge of my acts? That which in my sight
May seem proper, in yours may not, it is true;
But, even had I sinned, by what right do you
Cast at me the first stone?

Paul.

No doubt you would try
To excuse your falsehood. Perhaps you'd deny
That falsehood.

Lea.

Why should I? Does your love then call
For such a denial? Are you certain, Paul,
That you still merit mine? Pray, which of us two
Was the first to break faith? Was it I?

Paul.

Not *you.*
Not *you*, oh, not *you*, no—it was *I*, of course,
Who first broke our vows. *I* was the first to force
Asunder those chains which bound us. And 'twas *I*
Who abandoned *you*. *I* was the first to fly
From my oath. You are right to despise me, for
'Twas betrayal most base that man ever saw.

Lea.

And, if all this were but to prove you?

Paul.

Indeed,
The idea is not new. It could but succeed.

Lea.

Rather ask your father.

Paul.

My father! 'twas he
Who drove you away?

Lea.

Yes. He could not see
Our love with our eyes.

Paul.

Lea, had you not sworn
To love me? Had you been true, no force had torn
Us apart.

Lea.

I was true, and that truth relied
On your faith. See how that faith stands when 'tis tried.

Paul.

'Twas a debt I owed to my father. But see
How *you* have kept *your* faith; for, no sooner free

From the chains of my love, you fly to the arms
Of another for comfort. You cast those charms
To the first man you meet. Another than I
Has shared in your passion. Oh fie, woman, fie!
Oh, without doubt, to you all men are the same.
Oh, shame on you, woman! Shame, deep, damning shame!
Down, down on your knees; ask pardon, if you can,
For your crime cries aloud, base, vile courtesan!
(*Seizes her violently by the arm, throws her at his feet, then starts back overwhelmed at his own violence.*)
Oh that my heart would break!

Lea.

Hear me speak, Paul.
'Twas the third of September; that day when all
That I prized had been lost.

Paul.

My wedding-day.

Lea.

Yes,
'Twas your wedding-day. In my sad distress
The news of it reached me; that news drove me mad.
I saw you bestow all those vows which you had
Sworn were mine on her. I saw her at that shrine
Where I should have stood. That great love which was mine
You gave her. I fell. Oh, think not I defend
That crime. If my despair could have made an end
Of my life, I had died. (*Pause.*)

Paul.

No, Lea, that crime
And that shame are not yours. No, Lea, they're mine.
I blame you no more; let the past be the past,
And let us forget it. Beloved one, at last
I can claim you again. (*Taking her in his arms.*)

Lea.

Release me !

Paul.

Once more
You are mine.

Lea.

Release me ! What, forget I swore
To drive you from my heart ! Never ! Here I swear
On my hope of heaven again (*Releasing herself.*)

Paul.

Then you dare
Defy me ?

Lea.

If I must ! I bid you farewell
For ever.

Paul.

You leave me ?

Lea.

Yes, Paul, you compel
Me to fly from you.

Paul.

You shall not. I forbid
You to stir. You shall not : no, you shall not. Did
You not swear to be mine ? And you shall.

Lea.

Away !

Paul.

Lea !

Lea.

Free me !

Paul.

Lea !

Lea.

Release me, I say ;
Would you resort to force ? (*Rings bell.*)

Paul.

Yield to me without
Or you'll drive me wild.

[*Enter James.*]

Lea (*to James*).

Show that gentleman out.

(*Lea stands pointing to the door. Paul, after a moment's hesitation, takes his hat and goes off slowly.*)

END OF ACT THIRD.

ACT FOURTH.

Same scene as First Act. Paul and John discovered packing a portmanteau.

Paul.

You must tell my father, the reason I am
Obliged to leave home is that a telegram
Has been sent me from Nice ; that my friend Reynal
Is very ill, and in a most critical
State.

John.

Poor Mr. Reynal ! It will much surprise
Your father, Mr. Paul.

Paul.

Yes, you must apprise
Him as gently as you can. Be sure you break
It to him by degrees, and let him not take
It too much to heart. I will write and tell why
I have had to go without saying goodbye.
If I were now to wait to see him again
I should certainly miss the ten o'clock train.
Comfort him, if you can.

John.

I'll try, Mr. Paul.

Paul.

There's something for yourself. (*Gives money.*)

John.

Thank you. Is that all?
Can I do nothing more?

Paul.

You may take these
Things down-stairs, and call me a cab, if you please.
[*Exit John.*]
Let them sleep on in peace; 'tis best they should not know
That I am gone, until my letter, by slow
Degrees, breaks the news. Like some thief in the night,
Like some base criminal, who, seeking by flight
To cover his guilt, makes that guilt but more deep,
Am I. Yet *am* I to blame? Why should I keep
Faith with them who have failed to keep faith with me?
Was this marriage not of their making? Did he,
My father, not force me into it? Should I
Have married Camille else? No, 'twas a base lie
When they called Lea false. Then why should I spare
Those who have not spared me? Why should I forbear
To punish their deceit? She was my first choice,
And to her arms I fly. Shall I heed the voice
Of conscience?—

[*Enter Forrester.*]
My father!

Forrester.

Why, how is this, Paul?
So poor Reynal's ill. John has just told me all
About it. I met him, just now, at the door,
In search of a cab, so I sent him off for
Your wife.

Paul.

But I—really have no time to spare.

Forrester.

Oh, you've plenty of time.

Paul.

Are you then aware
That the train goes at ten ?

Forrester.

And it is only eight.
There's not the least danger that you'll be too late.
Camille will soon arrive,—I am much surprised
Reynal sent for you, for you never disguised
Your own dislike for him ; but then I suppose
He did not perceive it. I would not oppose
His dying request. And 'tis well that you go
Just now.

Paul.

Ah, indeed !—

Forrester.

For Lea's sake.

Paul.

Why so ?

Forrester.

I imagined I saw—no doubt I was wrong—
That she'd not forgotten.

Paul.

What, and it is so long
Since she went away—full six months!

Forrester.

True, but how
She opposed my wishes !

Paul.

Did she really now ?

Forrester.

Well, I conquered at last.

Paul.

So I've heard.

Forrester.

Then you know
All about it ?

Paul.

I do.

Forrester.

'Tis she—

Paul.

Even so—
'Tis she who has told me.

Forrester.

Then you must confess
Our plan has succeeded, and our great success
Justifies our means, does it not ?

Paul.

I suppose
It does. But, when a man's at my age, he knows
His own mind commonly. Those who interfere
Do so at their own risk.

Forrester.

Did you see her here,
Or at her own home ?

Paul.

At her house ; I went
But in Adolph's behalf ; to gain her consent
To their marriage.

Forrester.

You urge *his* claim? You possess
An unselfish heart, Paul. Did she consent?

Paul.

Yes.

Forrester.

I rejoice sincerely.

Paul.

I knew that you would.
(*Seeing Adolph, who is looking in at the door.*)

Forrester.

Pray come in; what is it?

Adolph.

Good day, Paul. (*To Forrester.*) Now could
You do me a favor?

Forrester.

Perhaps; let me hear
What it is.

Adolph.

I'm in love.

Forrester.

Again!

Adolph.

Yes, Lea
Has at last won my heart.

Forrester.

At last, are you sure?

Adolph.

I can't live without her.

Forrester.

And do you think your
Love will last?

Adolph.

Forever. I swear it!

Forrester.

Paul tells
Me you asked for his help.

Adolph.

Yes, but he compels
Me to ask yours now.

Forrester.

Did he refuse?

Adolph.

What use
To deny; he told me to go to the deuce.
(*To Paul.*) Did you not?

Paul.

I forget.

Adolph.

So, I went alone,
And asked her to have me.

Forrester.

With what luck?

Adolph.

I own
That I think she loves me. She did not say no;
But she did not say yes.

Forrester.

So, Paul would *not* go
Himselt?

Paul.

At first I refused ; then I changed my mind
And went to her after.

Forrester.

Are you sure ?

Adolph.

How kind
Of you, Paul !

Paul.

Not at all.

Adolph.

Did she then consent ?

Paul.

Not exactly.

Adolph.

Oh dear ! But she will repent.

(*To Forrester.*)

If *you* will intercede she cannot refuse.
I'm sure you will help me.

Forrester.

I will ; but excuse
Me at present—to-morrow—

Adolph.

To-morrow's too late,
She leaves at ten to-night ; it's now half-past eight.

Forrester.

At ten ! where's she going ?

Adolph

I think she said Nice.
Paul is to see her off ?

Forrester.

So! so! You increase
My desire to serve you, and, if it were not
That events keep me just now chained to this spot,
I would go. I can write.

Adolph.

It's no use to write;
For I tell you that she leaves Paris to-night.

Forrester.

Then I'll follow her.

Adolph.

What?

Forrester.

Yes, by the next train.

Adolph.

How kind!

Forrester.

Now, be off.

Adolph.

But how kind!

Forrester.

Once again,
Be off.

Adolph.

Good night, then. (*Aside*). Now I really cannot see
Why he should take such a great interest in me. [*Exit*].

Forrester (to Paul).

Now we're once more alone, let me see, my son,
Reynal's telegram.

Paul.

You know I've received none.

Forrester.

I suspected as much, but still was in doubt.
My soul could not credit such baseness without
Further proof.

Paul.

You have it.

Forrester.

You dare thus to fly
From your wife and from me ? You dare thus defy
The laws of God and man ? You dare cast such shame
On your true, young wife ? You dare blast my fair name
With such crime ? Are you without pity for her ;
For her fond, loving heart ? Did no remorse stir
Your heart in this deed ?

Paul.

What have I to do
With remorse ? Leave remorse to others. 'Tis you
Who speak of remorse ? You, who speak of her love ?
Have *I* then no heart ? Must *I* then perforce prove
My love by this act ? Was it not you who came
Between Lea and me ? Who else can I blame
For her falsehood but you ? But Lea's still true
To her love ; she's not false. as you hoped. Mark you,
I love Lea still, and love Lea alone,
Alone, do you hear me ? Have I not shown
More candor than you when I tell you that I
Now live only for her, and for her would die ?
For she has my whole heart Oh, why did you come
Between that love and me ? Could you not feel some
Pity ? But your love of yourself was more deep
Than your pity. As you've sown so shall you reap !

Forrester.

I accept your reproach. But admit, my son,
The fact, that what is done cannot be undone.

Paul.

But it can, and it shall.

Forrester.

Beware, Paul, beware !

Paul.

Would you threaten me, then ?

Forrester.

My son, have a care
What you say. Can it be that you've lost all sense
Of honor ? If that humor be not pretence,
I charge you to pause.

Paul.

So that the trick you've played
May not bear its just fruits ! No, rather than aid
Such deceit, I will cast all honor aside.

Forrester.

Then hear my firm resolve. This act does divide
Us forever. You are no longer my son.
I disown you as such. Henceforth I have one
Child only, and I shall know how to protect
Her against you as a stranger ; nor expect
Any mercy for me.

Paul.

I ask none. I cast
Your defiance back at you. So then, at last,
I see what you would do. You would interpose
Between Lea and me again, and, who knows,
Persuade her to marry Adolph. By that act
You would slay your own son.

Forrester.

'Tis well ; I exact
Retribution from you. To spare this disgrace

I would gladly see you die before my face.
(*Taking pistols from case and offering one to Paul.*)
Here I give you the means ; and now let me see
If you prefer honor or base infamy.

Paul.

I reject your offer. Nor did I expect
So blood-thirsty a one. 'Tis done for effect,
No doubt, but the Comedy's quite out of place.
We are not actors.

Forrester.

My son, spare this disgrace
To my gray hairs. Think, what can I say to her,
To Camille, when you're gone ?

Paul.

Be the minister
Of comfort yourself. Why, was she not your choice ?
She was none of mine ! 'Twould be strange if your voice
Could not bring her comfort.

Forrester.

You will kill her.

Paul.

No.
She'll live through it, *I* have.

Forrester.

How little you know
Of her great love for you !

Paul.

Then, pray, why not lend
Your aid to my plan. By your theory the end
Justifies the means. Why not let her believe
I am gone to Raynal ?

Forrester.

And help to deceive
Her confiding heart? What, Sir, you would see
Me a willing partner in your infamy?

Paul.

As you will; let me pass.

Forrester (*standing across the door*).

Paul, you shall not go,
You shall not desert us; no, I swear it, no.
You shall strike me down first.

Paul (*sitting down*).

Well, if I must wait
I *must* wait, that is all. If I should be late
For this train I can take the next.

Forrester.

Oh, my son,
Has it then come to this? What thing have we done
To bring down this judgment? No, it cannot be,
It is some dreadful dream. I his father, he
My son, my darling? Is it his voice I hear?
Is it mine that responds? Oh, surely my ear
Deceives me. No, 'tis true. You're free to depart.
Go your way! You have broken your father's heart.
(*Sinks into a chair, with his head in his hands.*)

Paul (*rising*).

Well, what must be must be. Now the die is cast
And I cannot draw back. This may be the last
Time we meet, my father. Farewell!

Camille (*outside.*)

Where is he?

[*Enter Camille.*]

Where is Paul?

Paul (*aside*).
Camille's voice !

Camille.
What has happened ?

Forrester (*starting up*).
See,
There the traitor stands.

Camille.
What mean you ?

Paul (*to Forrester*).
Are then you
Without pity for her ?

Forrester.
He flies.

Camille (*to Paul*).
Is this true ?

Forrester.
He elopes with Lea.

Camille.
Say, Paul, is this true ?
Speak. You are silent ? (*Sinks into chair.*)
What have I done to you,
That you should desert me ?

Forrester.
So, then, you still love
Him, my unhappy child ?

Camille.
I love him ! Above
All else in this world or the next. But, Paul, what

Have I done to deserve this thing ? Have I not
Been a true, loving wife ? Has it come to this
That you can desert me, that you can dismiss
My love from your heart ? What fault has been mine
That you should use me thus ; that you should resign
Me for her ? You never have loved me ; oh no,
You never have loved me. You are free to go.
You have my permission. I'll not interfere ;
You are free to depart. Go, fly with Lea,
If you will.

Forrester.

My poor child!

Camille.

No, pity me not.
He is dead to me now, and I have forgot
All the past ; let it die. The aim of my life
Has been to serve him, and I yield.

Forrester (*taking her in his arms.*)

But this strife
With yourself will kill you, my poor child.

Camille.

Well, so
Let it be.

Forrester (*to Camille*).

See, he yields.

Camille.

Then 'tis I will go.
I will not stand in their way, and should it kill
Me, what matters it ?

Paul.

Do with me as you will.

[*Exit.*]

Forrester.

You have conquered ; he yields.

Camille.

No, father, not so.
He has conquered : I yield. He is free to go.

[*Enter John.*]

Forrester.

Well, what is it you want ?

John.

Sir, Madame de Clers
Is down-stairs, and has asked to see you.

Forrester.

She dare
Come into this house!

Camille.

She is welcome.

Forrester.

At such
A time as this ! Oh, this is really too much.
(*To John.*) Say that I am engaged.

Camille.

Then I will receive
Her myself. Show her up. [*Exit John.*]

Forrester.

Camille ?

Camille.

You must leave
Me alone with Lea.

Forrester.

What would you do ?

Camille.

She
Comes to rob me of Paul. Now Lea shall see
That her love is less unselfish than mine.

Forrester.

Stay !

Camille.

Not a word !

Forrester.

But, Camille.

Camille.

No, leave me !

Forrester.

I obey.

[*Exit.*]

[*Enter Lea.*]

Lea.

What a strange reception ! Camille, let me know
If I am in the way.

Camille.

I who loved you so !

Lea.

Why, Camille, how is this ? I declare you all
Seem to fear my approach.

Camille.

You would fly with Paul.
Deny it if you can.

Lea.

And I do deny
It.

Camille.

You see he's ready.

Lea.

Camille, I defy
You to prove your charge. If Paul is resolved
To commit this great crime, I must be absolved
From any share in it ; for I have refused
To listen to him. 'Tis you who have accused
Me of this ! Oh, Camille, how little you know
My love for you both. Could you then think me so
Ungrateful ? But no, you do not understand
What there is in my heart. Camille, take my hand ;
Take it without fear ! 'tis honest.

Camille.

I believe
You, Lea, for I love you. You could not deceive
Me now, I am certain.

Lea.

The battle was hard ;
But the battle is won : I have my reward.

Camille.

To what do you refer ? Ah, yes, now I see ;
You love Paul.

Lea.

No, Camille.

Camille.

You *have* loved him.

Lea.

He
Is nothing to me.

Camille.

Ah ! I see it all now ;
Just heaven forgive me ! Oh, dear Lea, how—
How blind have I been, that I failed to perceive

All your self-sacrifice. Oh, yes, I believe,
For 'tis sweet to believe, that you love him not.
How noble have you been thus to have forgot
All your own hopes for me. It is only I
Who have stood in your way? Why, Lea, oh why
Should I stand in your way! You have both good right
To curse me, Lea. Now I see that your flight
Was to shun temptation. Oh, can you forgive
Me for what I have done? Why should I thus live
To be his curse and yours? How sweet 'twere to die
With your united love; and to feel that I
Passed away with your blessing, with your pity,
And knowing at last that I had set him free!

Lea.

How I worship you! How I despise him now;
You shall win him again.

Camille.

Never.

Lea.

I know how
To make him hate me.

Camille.

But, Lea, will that hate
Make him love me the more? Oh, no, 'tis too late.
What is it you would do?

Lea.

That's my secret.

Camille.

No,
Tis too late. Would you serve me still? Wait below
Till I come.

Lea.

I will wait. [*Exit.*]

Camille.

And now to prepare
Then for the last blow. I have no time to spare.

(*She hastily puts on her bonnet and cloak; writes a few lines and folds and places them on Paul's valise, which lies on a chair*).

Camille.

Farewell, my beloved home ; farewell, my bright
Dreams.

[*Enter Forrester.*]

Forrester.

Are you going out at this time of night ?

Camille.

Lea waits me down-stairs.

Forrester.

What for ?

Camille.

I can't tell
You now, I am in haste.

Forrester.

Camille, you compel
Me to suspect your acts, (*sees note*) your writing ! You fly
From my roof (*rings*).

Camille.

No, father.

Forrester.

Then what means this ?

Camille.

I—

I have an appointment.

[*Enter John.*]

Forrester (*to John.*)

Ask Paul to come here.

[*Exit John*].

Camille.

What would you do, father?

Forrester.

I've no right, 'tis clear,
To open your letters, of course, but I'll see
That this reaches Paul safely.

Camille.

Father, give me
Back my note.

Forrester.

No, Camille.

Camille.

For Paul's sake, restore
It me.

Forrester.

No.

Camille.

On my knees I ask it.

Forrester.

No more!

[*Enter Paul.*]

Paul.

You've sent for me, sir.

Forrester.

I've sent for you because
Camille flies from us. This will explain the cause.
(*Gives note.*)

Paul (reading).

" Dear Paul. Marry Lea ! 'Tis my dying prayer ;
And take my last blessing : " Great Heaven !

Camille.

Paul, there
Is no more peace for me, now I know that I
Stand between you and her. Dear Paul, let me die !
(*Paul falls overcome on his knees with his head in his hands.*)

Forrester.

You have conquered at last, my child,
(*Puts his hand on Paul's forehead and turns his head back.*) Camille, see
These tears on his cheek.

Camille.

They are tears of pity,
Not of love.

Forrester.

You still doubt ?

Camille.

I do. Until now
He has not loved me. May I trust such love ?

Forrester.

How
Can you judge of his heart ? There is only One
Great searcher of hearts. So let His will be done !
You may trust in him now.

Paul.

Camille, I've no right
To ask you to trust me. My wife, this contrite
Heart asks but forgiveness. Can you then forgive
All the wrong it has done? I ask but to live
In your presence, Camille. My wife, do not cast
Me out from your life.

Camille (after a pause).

Let the past be the past.
'Tis dead and gone now.

Paul (kneeling before Camille).

Thy mercy endures
For ever. Oh, woman, this mission is yours.

Adolph (at the door).

May we come in?

Forrester.

Of course.

[*Enter Adolph and Lea.*]

Adolph.

Pray, let me present
My wife—that is to be.

Forrester.

When is the event
To take place?

Adolph.

To-morrow.

Camille (going to Lea).

How can I repay
The debt I owe you?

Lea (embracing her).

You owe me nothing.

Camille.

Stay,
I owe you my husband.

Lea.

I owe you mine, thus
All our debts are paid.

Forrester.

Nay, who is there of us
That has paid all his debts ? So long as we live
Our debts surround us ; those blessings we receive
We cannot all repay. For all that we have
We have incurred debt : from our birth to our grave.
To our parents, our friends, to the world at large
We all owe a debt, not easy to discharge.
Of all our debts, there is but one we can pay ?
Tis the debt we owe na ture ; and when that day,
That awful day, comes, may we then not forget
How much there is needed to pay that great debt.

END OF ACT FOURTH.

THE NEW YORK PRINTING COMPANY,
205, 207, 209, 211, 213 EAST 12TH STREET.

www.ingramcontent.com/pod-product-compliance
Lightning Source LLC
LaVergne TN
LVHW021429110826
845150LV00007B/2149

* 9 7 8 1 4 2 5 5 0 7 2 1 3 *